Frank M. Chipasula

WHISPERS IN THE WINGS

New and Selected Poems

MALLORY PUBLISHING

Published by
Mallory Publishing,
Aylesbeare Common Business Park,
Exmouth Road,
Aylesbeare,
Devon,
EX5 2DG,
England

For a complete list of titles, visit
http://www.mallorypublishing.co.uk
e-mail: admin@mallorypublishing.co.uk

First published in this form 2007 by Mallory Publishing
Copyright © Frank M. Chipasula 1991, 2007

First published by Heinemann International Literature and Textbooks in 1991 ISBN 0435 91192 9 Some previously published poems came out of the following books: Nightwatcher, Nightsong (Paul Green, 1986), O Earth, Wait for Me (Ravan Press, 1984) and journals.

ISBN-10 1 85657 108 4
ISBN-13 978 1 85657 108 1

Cover design © Mallory International Limited 2006

All rights reserved. No part of this publication may be reproduced, stored in a retrieval system, or transmitted in any form or by any means, electronic, mechanical, photocopying, recording or otherwise, without the prior permission of the publishers.

The right of Frank M. Chipasula to be identified as the author of this work has been asserted by him in accordance with the copyright, designs and patents act 1988.

FRANK M. CHIPASULA is a Malawian poet, editor and fiction writer, born on 16 October 1949. He holds a B.A. (with Credit) from the University of Zambia, an M.A. in Creative Writing from Brown University, an M.A. in Afro-American Studies from Yale University and a Ph.D. in English Literature from Brown University. Currently an Associate Professor and Judge William Holmes Cook Professor of Black American Studies at Southern Illinois University in Carbondale, he has also taught at Howard University, Tamkang University in Tamsui, Taiwan, University of Nebraska at Omaha, St. Olaf College in Northfield, Minnesota, as well as Brown and Yale Universities. He also worked as English Editor for NECZAM Ltd., the former national publishers of Zambia in Lusaka and, as an undergraduate student at the University of Malawi, he freelanced on the M.B.C. (Malawi Broadcasting Corporation) in Blantyre, Malawi.

Chipasula's first book, Visions and Reflections *(1972), was a pioneering work in English by a Malawian poet and paved the way for* O Earth, Wait for Me *(1984) and* Nightwatcher, Nightsong *(1986). He has also edited the following ground-breaking anthologies of African poetry:* When My Brothers Come Home: Poems from Central and Southern Africa *(Wesleyan University Press, 1985), (with Stella)* The Heinemann Book of African Women's Poetry *(Heinemann 1995) and* Bending the Bow: An Anthology of African Love Poetry *(forthcoming). His poems have appeared in numerous literary journals, newspapers and anthologies in Africa, Europe, the USA and Asia in English, French, Spanish and Chinese.*

Mallory Classic African Writing

An Introduction to the Series

Mallory International is one of the leading exporting booksellers in the United Kingdom, and works particularly in Africa, where our customers include many Ministries of Education, Universities, and other institutions.

We have found from experience that many classic works by African writers are out of print, or no longer available, and this series is intended to remedy that situation, making available for ongoing distribution a range of titles, both fiction and non-fiction, which might otherwise disappear.

I hope you enjoy this book. If you do, and you are aware of another important title which could usefully be reprinted, please contact us. E-mail addresses and contact details can be found on our web site.

Julian Hardinge,
Chairman,
Mallory International

Contents

Zikomo ix
Dedication xi

I from Nightwatcher, Nightsong 3
I Dusk 4
from III Dawn 6

II The Flowers of Malawi 9
The Flowers of Malawi 10
Flowering Wounds 12
A Monument to a Tyrant 14
In the Field of Pain 17
In the Garden of Fire 18
Tyrants, Listen! 19
A Poem for Martyrs' Day 20
Nightfall 21
Nightmare 22
Chilobwe 23
The Flood of Nineteen-Seventy 24
The New Masquerades 25
The Modern Beggars 26
To the Praise Dancers 27
In the Land of Sour Milk and Bittersweet Honey (I) 28
In the Land of Sour Milk and Bittersweet Honey (II) 29
Those Makheta Nights 31
Going Back Patiently 33
A Love Poem for my Country 34
A Hanging 35
Walking Under a Tall Building 38
A Grain of Salt 41
The Dark Veil 44
Singing Like Parrots 45
Again, the Dagger Speaks 46
The Emperors for Life 47
The Bitter Onions 48
The Birds of State 50

In the House of Power 51
Pot Bellies and Swollen Cheeks 53
My Aunt's Tales 54
Matiningale 55
The Singing Drum 57

The Strange Graves 59

The Killing Grounds 60
Wiriyamu 63
Nhazonia 66
Shrapnel 67
The Burning Rose 69
Madonnas and Children 70
The Orphan Boy of Kampala 72
Soweto Child 73

Atlantic Crossing 75

Atlantic Crossing 76
Farewell Street 78
God's Acre 79
This Island Now 80
Wizard 82
Night Exodus 84
In Exile 85
Ukimbizi 86
Ode to a Congo Pygmy in the Bronx Zoo 87
Requiem for an African Woman in a Glass Case in Paris 88
Ebony Root 89
Tikambepo 91
A Crane from Home 92

Finale 93

Manifesto on Ars Poetica 94
We Must Crush the Parasite 95

Acknowledgements 97

Zikomo

To *Greg Gatenby, Artistic Director of the Reading Series at The Harbourfront in Toronto, Canada, for an opportunity to read with some of the finest contemporary poets in the April 1990 World Poetry Festival and for the typewriter which enabled me to begin work on this book. I know some are asking, 'What is Chipasula doing?' I have been here, in my warm little hole, tuning my crude guitar and preparing to blossom into new songs. And when I stagger under the burden of these songs, I hope you will be there to give me a hand as you did during that reading which revived my faith in poetry.*

F.M.C.

for Helen and Masauko
May you always walk in the great light.

THE POEMS

I

NIGHTWATCHER,

Nightsong

◊

I have not come to make wars on earth
but to pick flowers
I am the singer-king who looks for flowers
Ernesto Cardenal

I *Dusk*

Nightwatcher:
Fast falls the night unfurling its vile veil
Showering its soot into our eyes plunging us into deep darkness
Extinguishing the fiery flame of the spent sun.
The sharp shrilling shrieks of the last detainees
Herded into dark catacombs of Mikuyu and Chingwe's Hole
Drown the maenadic frenzy of the ululating chorus bitches
Brandishing party cards, passports to feasting houses
As dust fills the crowing cock's mouth taking it for dawn:
Then death goes hunting through men's huts with long knives.

Nightwatcher:
Carrion birds dig and probe with their erect lethal beaks
Into the Chibuku-beer drenched bodies of the chorus bitches
Hawking genitals, stirring, inflaming their lust for farms, cars,
Houses, plane-rides into a frenzy of butt-wriggling dances.
At the sumptuous midnight banquets for the devil
The cantors parrot praise songs and slogans
As the ferocious tame leonine Messiah rides the death chariot
Stirring the coarse dust of dissent with his wicked horse-tail.

Nightwatcher:
These streets are tired and drowsy, sleepless feet drag heavy chains,
Lamp-posts weep under the cold dead weight of the crimson dew
Condensed out of the flow from the feet pierced by sharp barbs
As they cudgel them through the nets into the House of Seven Locks
While the deep nightfall veils the secret murders in its shroud,
Muffles the painful wails of the bereaved wives, mothers and children,
Knits our brows with beeswax and drugs us into submissive stupor
Like bees smoked in our tree-cave hideouts and dark dungeons.

Nightwatcher:
The dwarfed despot descends his lofty ivory throne of polished bones,
Dips into the bathtub filled with human blood,
Splashes frantically for the saving straw, sinks slowly into the quagmire

Drunk on the bitter champagne of tears from battered babies;
From the chalice of a polished human skull he drinks,
The great lion devoid of leonine mercy mauls his own,
With the song of the screech owl and the nightjar in his ears.

Nightwatcher:
The same teeth that threatened to rip the enemy now smile
At the same men as their arms gather and embrace him intimately
The same hands that wielded home-made guns and poisoned arrows
Tremble as they shake our foe with the tender warmth of our milked land
The same feet that ran and chased the master out of our country
Now strut on the platforms in the thick boots left by master.
With these they are tearing the mouths of our people, their new enemy.

Nightwatcher, fear is dexterously woven like a dredge net
That tightens its dry iron meshes around each hut
Pain-laden voices escape through the cracked doors and
Spread their blood-tinted gossamer all over the slumbering land.
The official claws are squeezing the dissenting throats
Until the vocal cords snap and the windpipes are totally crushed,
The voices muzzled and the reed flutes discarded, their sweet song stolen.
Fear has chained them to a boulder that hangs dangerously over them.

Nightwatcher:
Authority passes its clenched fist through the people's minds
Feeling for the sharp edges of divergent thought
Uniting millions of survival champions of the world
Who have to lie to keep alive from the zealous knobkerries
Of the over-patriotic thugs driving our country into brewing storms.

Nightwatcher, ten thousand citizens enmeshed in barbed-wire nets!
Abroad our ambassadors rant and boast about our peace and calm
While at home we dance on fire and bruise our backs on thorns:
Fawners crawl, prostrate themselves before the despot,
Lick his boots, polish his ass with their long tongues,
Scramble for fallen crumbs under perpetual banquet tables
Praising our chief executioners brandishing gory daggers.

from III Dawn

Nightwatcher:
You hold ajar the heavy gates of time
And in floods the tattered continuous past like a tumultuous river.
Centuries gore-smeared bows, arrows and spears itching for battle
Razed lands and cannon smoke rising in troubled spirals
Chains that gripped tightly a whole people's soft minds, crumbling.
The past embraces a secret as dark as your form, Nightwatcher,
The old year has folded his mats and gone limping away
Sulking into the thickets of darkness, greying to the skin.
Let our gore swell your angry waters, Nightwatcher, that we may swamp
Those plump-cheeked giants riding dwarfed brothers like hyenas.

Flood, of blood, of my people, wait for me — surge!
The night is breathing into dawn, its anger steaming.

Matsakamula,
You carry the heavy loads of thunder into the distance
Crushing the already collapsing huts in this tired night
Your back, a long fiery trail of lightning;
You shed torrential tears of rain, your own fire scorching you:
As your tears labour to put out the tongues of fire
Licking your granaries, the great divine fight still raging on,
Mphambe sends his bow of many colours arching across your anguish
To fold your bags of rain while our cities and villages
Are soundly sleeping, though a dark and violent claw gnaws
At our opulent dreams, intruding upon our hopes of huge yields:

Nightwatcher:
When day dawns, that calm slumbering lake caressing our country
Will rise up dancing violently on its tail, teeth bared ruthlessly, charging
And I will bathe with my people in its raging flames, stretching my wings
Wide, soaring high through tongues of fire licking my skin and flesh
Down to the enduring core, my spirit emerging pure, moulted
out of the dirt.

¤ ¤ ¤

Nightwatcher, the gentle night whispers to you a new song
that fills your heart till you are song
spilling into the fading night, impregnating it till
its swollen womb strains to burst and burst wide open
in a pool of bloody violent light and delayed day
gives out its first victory cry rending the shrouded sky.

Nightwatcher, as you crack your hot molten whip
On this dark lake, give me one last speck of light
Light this dark path out of this long and perilous night:
Under your whip let each sinister wave turn upon itself,
Inflict pain on its own aqueous body, and maul its own stinging tail.

¤ ¤ ¤

Nightwatcher:
I beat my spear-point on your solid aged anvil
And whet its blade on the lip of the whirlwind,
The tail of the hurricane, the blade of the cyclone —
Flash your potent fiery lightning on its firm tongue,
Ignite its blade into a sharp scorching flame
That I may rip the cloaking veil of darkness and hate
Off the hooded face of our raped mutilated land
And tattoo love on her belly and sweet secret places.

I will speak with the long tongue of lightning,
Growl with the roll of a million drums of thunder
That distant murmur of tremulous earthquake
That sudden routing bolt of thick hot lightning.

I come in the solid flesh of your muscular dreams:
I will resurrect the gaunt sun from its sickbed
And scatter this darkness with one flaming sword of light.

Lusaka, Zambia: 1976-78

II

THE FLOWERS OF MALAWI

◊

The polished skulls bloom
into a corolla of light
from which the nectar of blood
drips under the blows of knobkerries
Frank M. Chipasula

In the land where hands are laid on the Bible
But the Bible is not opened.
David Diop

The Flowers of Malawi

A primal spark from the sun — and the fire flowered:
The early morning blossoms
bobbed serenely on the golden
waves where the first fire flowered.

The subtle tongue of the sun
fed the spark from the steel
bar of the barbed-wire cage.
It raged and sliced the flowers'
dreams in two: half a nightmare,
half a dream contending for half
a body, and sleep was sliced too.

The steel blade sliced cleanly off
the heads of the sad sunflowers:
The fire flowered on the forge also
its flame tapered into a sword blade
that wagged from Chitipa to Nsanje,
Mchinji to Likoma Island, and
clipped the corolla of the sunflowers.

And when the shrieks sliced the night,
it bled the news into the widows' eyes
searching for their decapitated zinnias
bullet-riddled, sad ministerial hibiscus
their stems totalled in a staged smash
below the escarpment along Chitawila Road.

Denying rumours of escape, the bemused
ministerial hearse stared through dimming head-
lamps while it coughed and retched blood.
And the surprised bodies searched
for their heads by the flame of independence
that blossomed in the rough-wood crates.

And the wounds gaped and kept their perpetual
eyes open, ripe as alligator pepper
watered by the chronic tears of the sun.

In the toy tyrant's hands
the flowers flamed, the fire flowered
in the reckless hands without brakes
to stop them from sowing the seeds of fire.

He slung the monstrous cornerstones at them:
'We are playing war, not cricket', waving
a bouquet of severed heads, his Nyasa-
Scottish tongue wagging in His Master's Voice.

The wives, handsome with their inconsolable
sorrow, gathered the jig-saw puzzle of those
flowers that plummeted dangerously
down the bitter centuries of servitude.

The adorable widows captured the blossoms
before they fled down the Naperi River and
pinned that sad flesh in the toy coffins.

Suddenly, the gaping wounds parted their lips
and laughed and retched, and the fable turned
the blood into a bird whose song covered the land,
covered the dawn with a leaden silence.

And when the beautiful widows hummed the news
in dirges, a deep echo resounded in Chile
and Argentina in their hands as they unwrapped
little tyrants in the dark cloth of the night
that blindfolded the moon and the stars
that blossomed in the pale morning light.

Northfield, MN: 14 November 1988

Flowering Wounds

Old wounds blossom
on the copper beach
and hiss with the heat
with the crash of the pounding
waves that garrison the island
their venomous stamens
claw at the peaceful
slumbering people's dreams.
The lake grips, wields
and dashes these gory
flowers, bleeds their pain
which bred us all
in these furious waves.
The lake's awakening anger
scalds the wounds with
perpetually open petals
and showers their poisonous
pollen on the pistils of the grey rock.
It bends away from the target
and extends to us a fiery corolla
of pollinated pain and lashes us
with a garland of hatred.
It clamps us in a tight embrace
that shrinks our minds
and bayonets our subversive thoughts
suddenly breaking into fruit.
The waves hammer flames till their petals
fire our veins and grind the bones
and pebbles of anger into pure flour
for the toughening porridge
and put a cutting edge to the whetstone
where the toy soldiers break their backs
as they spread the dark counterpane of curfew
over our peaceful silent island.
As they pound the island with their heavy

boots and bayonet the flowering waves,
they shoot flames into the sweet water
that blooms blooms blooms until the copper-
beach blossoms and blossoms with
the old wounds that open and bloom.

3 March 1983

A Monument to a Tyrant

And, when he cried, the little children died in the streets

W. H. Auden

Draw a tiny iron-fisted tyrant
Out of the iron-ribbed rock
As Michelangelo released
The human spirit embedded in marble:
On Fools Day unchain him,
Enchain him and erect him,
Imprison him in concrete
In a moribund monument
And set him naked by the roadside
At the mercy of Chiperoni whips,
Icy whips and herdboys' sjamboks:
A spitoon for the weary traveller,
A receptacle for bird-lime: *Chimbudzi!*[1]

In this concrete imprison all the mess,
the chaos, brutality, the torture:
Our History.
Harden the concrete around the steel hand
that has gripped and strangled our land,
The ruthless strokes of his dreaded pen
on the scarred skin of the detainee.
Let his hallucinations and paranoia
stand like a frieze on his cold bronze face
and in the pale metallic eyes gazing
frightfully at the mythic lizard
permanently imprinted on his mind's wall.

His heart will turn colder
and sink into his heavy feet:
Let his vicious thoughts congeal there
His motion arrested in the stone
As he flees his own sinister shadow.

Let his blunt hatred find
its deep carve there
in the iron-ribbed rock:
Mix the concrete with his victims' blood
Let his form itself rest
on the terrible crucifix of his sin,
hanging there, this — his meed —

Imprison in the bronze
his eye's evil glitter and crocodile smile.
Let the light and song of the poet
and the fatal fall of the sculptor's hand
reveal this fiend to the world:
'Let us give unto Caesar
his brutality, his heartlessness'.

Raise it so his brutality
towers over the little good he did —
Let his iron hand, under which
thousands have perished, show through
the cold concrete and stone.
And let the concrete freeze
and hold his tyranny
to posterity, his eagle-eye
and claw, his steel beak
that picked our land clean
clearly accented, unhidden,
and inscribe in blood
all the names of the innocent
victims crushed under his regime.
The iron-ribbed rock stretches forth
its terrible claws,
offers us tiny concrete cell blocks,
walls crowned with barbed wire,
bares its hideous, obscene
and monstrous face where victories
inflicted against his own people frieze

inscribed in golden letters:
DZELEKA, AUSCHWITZ,
BUCHENWALD, MIKUYU, TULE LAKE:
The iron fingers fold round necks
and snap them like flower buds . . .

Frieze the dis-ease and the brewing
storm in the iron-ribbed rock,
in the conduits of hatred
elemental and base, onerous
bronze age of the dead rabbit-eye,
the fiendish eyesore that I saw —
bleeding blade and weeping stone:
the bloody, bowed rainbow days
loaded with dynamite and crystalline tears.
Let the icy hand grip him
and freeze him into his concrete block
sculpted in his own image,
gnawed by the tooth of the chisel,
tortured and driven by anger,
braided and seasoned with hatred.
Let the icy arrow rip through his cannibal
heart and fill it with the final cold.

And thus dethroned by death,
let him stand there lonely
despotic, tyrant till . . .

New Haven: 27 July 1981

---

[1]*Chimbudzi*   Nyanja for toilet

In the Field of Pain

I step into the field of pain again,
Into the sweet dance of pain that sweetens
My anger, and feast on the sweet flames
That lick me clean again as they burn
The sweet slogans the flag cock has spewed
Out of its mouth filled with a gory sunset.

In the field I gather the toasted flowers
Before they toss them into the hungry rivers
Where they dump our surplus unmourned lives.
I reach for the darkened cell and yank the door:
Behind, the bagged flowers groan, suffocating

As their mouths are packed with darkness,
The daily diet of ignorance, the lean ration
Of praise songs beneath the threat of the baton.
In the cell of pain the flowers rage and rage
And rage until they choke on their own anger.

Toronto: 4 April 1990

In the Garden of Fire

This is the same garden of fire
that he sowed, against which he now
turns the spears, bows and arrows.
And when he touches us with a spearpoint
sharp as the torrential tropical rain
we crumble in his trained surgical hands;
Yet with sweet songs we fill our bellies
with sugar-coated slogans while our famished
feet feast on debauched ceremonial dances
while he pierces our eyes with horsehair
till, blinded, we dance into trap-ditches
where concealed fires lick what is left
of our clay into cold useless ash lugged
and tipped nightly into Namitembo River
where the overflooding blood clots us together
for one more day of waiting and buying time.
And we dance ourselves again into false safety
as we patiently watch him finish his thirty-year
project of crushing us lovingly between his iron
fingers of spears, bows and arrows that rain
on the body of a land he has loved to death,
where he planted the fiery flowers
in that night before the first dawn.
This is that same garden of fire blossoming.

Toronto: 5 April 1990

Tyrants, Listen!

Our land is drunk on blood now;
Her eyes are peppery red, her thighs sunken in gore,
Her breasts filled, almost bursting, with
Blood! Like a sponge thirsty for youthful blood,
Like a vampire crazed for blood,
Like a tycoon, a dealer in plasma and flesh,
She sits at the banqueting table and
Guzzles and guzzles pots of blood.
Now demented, she chases after budding boys,
wrings their necks, snaps them and collects the sap.
Listen tyrants, we have turned her into a drunkard.

17 June 1989

A Poem for Martyrs' Day

The first vowel of pain
pierces the night, O!

We recoil in our nightmares,
hearing a man scream like a goat

under a merciless knife.
The cry coils about the midnight
pitch darkness, out of Chingwe's

Hole and Mikuyu Prison Farm.
It strikes our hearts like a Black

Mamba crested with a deadly moon,
a rainbow of blood draped over
the bowed moon's hidden arrow.

The hills are aflame with dirges,
the valleys sob silently, afraid
of Special Branch ears —

The shock waves spread like
hot butter on this stale land.

The psalms raise the alms in the burnt
incense of dark human flesh
in the dawn of Palm Sunday.

Martyrs' Day: All quiet — the night's
Murders well hushed. All quiet.

Nightfall

for Jack Mapanje

In the sad hotel that drinks a swamp,
You breathe malarial air and enjoy
Frog music piped in from the dismal swamp.

Bits of your life measured out in bars,
Your thoughts gripped in clamps,
Your lips pierced through

With fish-hooks, locked shut,
Silenced over the stab of a clipped
Tongue that stabs the steel bar clutching

The teeth gnashed for dinner.
You dunk salt balls into the soup
Of bitter tears raging through our land.

Fried cockroaches, rotten beans
Baked in the perennial salt
Whet your old ulcerous hunger

As you journey from nowhere to nowhere
Stopping at the sad hotel that offers
No respite to despotic tyranny.

For many years you have silently swallowed
The bitter cassava of tyranny
Served to you at dagger-point.

Now, at nightfall, you muster your bitter
Breath brewing in your belly a storm
That will blow down the night at dawn.

Northfield: 1988

Nightmare

Darkness chained me to my tattered reed mat;
The hand of tyranny sprinkled
The soot of ignorance in my eyes, and sleep
Hammered my head with slogans,
Then a nightmare stumbled on my sprawled life,
Tripped on the alarm of my heart,
And set me singing a healing song.

With song I bandage my ravaged land;
With the thread of song I sew the chopped heads
Back on the shoulders of the plucked flowers.
I plug the neck gash with a war chant;
With a sharp spear whose tongue sings,
I rip the veil of darkness from our land,
And the nightmare flees my secret light.

18 September 1984

Chilobwe

Some drunken god is thirsty for blood again;
Dionysius of the revels, perhaps, that scoundrel god?
He has sent a darkness creeping all over our land
like a deadly poisonous vine showering its venom,
And death, the combine harvester, sank
his sharp discs into its flesh;
Blood axes dealt blows to her nape,
the petals of blood spread out like morning glory
And the blood banks neatly tubed to its slit veins
collect the honey for export to Joni in nightly planes.

Mothers hug deflated dugs slowly distending,
like cow udders, with funeral dirges unsung
under the iron hand that wields the scythe
that beheads their sweet little children.
What was the dagger looking for in their necks
where it left the tattoo marks under the heavy
torrential blows of the blunt knobkerie,
where the skin budded out, burst and bloomed,
blood blossoming on the burning calyx of sorrow
bedewed with pearly tears of the bereaved.

The clipped syllables of hatred above the angry whispers;
They nipped the bloom off the bullet-riddled stalks
With sharpened machetes and sealed the necks.
A rain of bullets drenched them in a swamp of blood
gushed from bashed chests and clipped genitals.

10 June 1983

The Flood of Nineteen-Seventy

Rhymed strangely with the blood
Napolo whipped out of the restless dust
That surged from neck veins neatly
Tubed to Pretoria by the night flights
In unregistered planes piloted by Boers
Coincident with the mass axe murders in Chilobwe.
The strangling chains tightened round our necks
The cannibal axe followed with its sharp tooth
Dancing and chewing through the edible flesh
Rejoicing at sumptuous banquets and cocktails:
The poor land is rich in blood, their bitter wine;
A million Malawian gallons polish diamonds:
It was among the first to burst apartheid's cordons
Resuscitating icy hearts and oiling machines.
Today, enormous leaves are sprouting
on Vorster's doorsteps where the waves lash.
The blood is weeping in South Africa: in Soweto —
It has slapped the monster's face in Malawi;
It sobs on the hands of the heart surgeons,
It cries among the coins of the tycoons and tyrants;
It writhes among the booty of the collectors and vendors
And the gluttonous middlemen of Lilongwe
And Zomba caught knee-deep in the gory swamp.
That flood left its terrible footprints on our history.

New Haven: Spring 1981

The New Masquerades

A masked dwarfed despot
teeters on stilts
clutching horse-hair
flywhisks whose sharp
hair cuts and lacerates
the disciples in the dust.
It is the third hour
of betrayal;
Hope has thrice beaten
its wings and crowed.
Among these hens a dark rooster
spits darkness like venom
into their eyes and the stars.
He scoops the honey
that wells from the earth,
and dances, masked still,
on his lofty stilts.

May 1990

The Modern Beggars

Dis-
Honorable jet-set beggars in three-piece suits
brandish their begging satchels filled
with shrivelled ten-year development plans
on yellowing recycled, cast-off paper —
Immaculate in their loaned silk ties,
dark goggles and wing-tipped brogues,
they toss base-metal coins into beggars' bowls
and pray for luck as they hop onto the jumbos
leashed to the metropolitan umbilical cord;
They suffer from tumultuous send-offs
on their annual begging missions for AID.
Tongues scraped raw from licking boots
for fallen crumbs at sumptuous banquets
where they are toasted on the blood we bled
and receive left-over and obsolete guns
with which they terrorize their own kinsfolk
who accord them heroes' welcomes on their return.

25 September 1988

To the Praise Dancers

The song foams at your mouth
While a sweat-drop perches on your nipple
Like a jewel or glass bead;
Your body is a flooding spring of song:
You fondle and squeeze your heart,
Inflate your bosom with song
Filled with your warm blood
To tickle the whims of your master
The roaring lion that prances on the platform,
The gaunt tyrannical messiah portraited
on your perennial dancing uniforms.
They have muzzled your voices and stuffed
Musty slogans into your patched throats
choking on the bilge of stale praise names.
Their songs blossom with poisonous petals
dagger-edged in the insulted air, murderous
in putrid pudenda flaunted in dance arenas.
Now mere bamboo baskets, you sieve moral water
between your haunches where maddened ministers
trash their rotten seed as they herd you
into whoredom, drunk on free Party Chibuku.
You wield your portraited passport
to banqueting stadia, your boarding pass
to jets bound for the metropole.

In the Land of Sour Milk and Bittersweet Honey
(I)

Where tyrants' hold is tightened,
Where strong devour the weak,
Where innocents are frightened
The righteous fear to speak . . .
from 'O Christ the Great Foundation'

In a land where sour milk
and bittersweet honey flow freely,
Ashen, soccer-ball bellied
Kwashiokor babies suck
a bitter honey that streams
out of their nostrils
and forage for breadcrumbs
in the tycoons' dustbins.
In the bars, hunched over counters,
Ex-detainees sip tears from gin tots,
while emaciated men line the streets
and make manacle music for
the passing heroes
back from begging missions,
and the fat-hipped women roast
on the red coals of lust
for the lavish hotel-dinners,
and in the bush, hawk-eyed
man-handlers entangled
in their own prisoners' chains
burn in their charges' sun
finger their triggers
as they watch grown men shit
Blood

2 May 1985

In the Land of Sour Milk and Bittersweet Honey
(II)

Beggars crawl along the streets
exhibiting their subversive poverty,
living on despair, wailing prayers
for alms, wallowing in the sweet
poisoned air.
In the rugged townships —
tattered Zingwangwa, blood-drenched
Chilobwe, or dishevelled Makheta —
people reel under stinging blows
of crude gin against their hashish heads,
chewed lungs and itchy sexes.
Lice-infested babies,
stuffed with mud pies,
scramble with dogs over crumbs
and mouldy chicken bones
on the rubbish heaps,
and take their morning bath
in the puddles of stale urine.
The shacks dressed in cardboards,
sacking and planks
from cast-off apple crates,
go begging
before refrigerated houses
veiled in air-conditioned
dreams
in Sunnyside where
fat dogs siesta on Alpo and dog
biscuits from London or New York.
In this land of sour milk
and bittersweet honey,
the true drums that spoke
fearlessly
have lost their tongues;

All that we hear now
is a single hoarse
and monotonous voice
as if
the whole country
had washed its hands,
folded up its arms
indifferently
and shut up its mouth:
One voice,
one demented voice
that is not tired of hearing
itself repeat the worn-out
middle-aged story
of a land brimming with
milk and honey.
All we hear now
is the senile voice
of a man who put stones
in detention
because they refused
to sing his praises, refused to sing
of flowing milk and honey.

1 July 1990

Those Makheta Nights

I heard the crude gin sobbing
in the Lactogen milk-can tots
in the rusty complaints of the creaking
bolts, hinges and the flapping iron
roofs yanked and toyed by the wind
like goat-skin bellows sharpening a flame
and the men mourning over it
strange winds neighing painfully
in a drop of the opaque Chibuku beer
trapped, suffocated in a decorated cardboard
packet to be shaken among
the long tongues of *kholoboyi*[1] lamps.
The long dry fingers of the winter plucked
the banjo and guitar wires, twisted our learned bellies
till they groaned and screamed with mustered bitterness
echoing the mysterious sobs of the gin's 'head'
flaming from the mud floor, intoxicated paper-thin
babies, their ribs mere accordions stretched
by the violent hands of perpetual hunger,
wailed their own dirges from their mothers' backs,
bulging eyes loaded with itchy sleep
wakeful at midnight, watching their mothers' flesh
melt in the discordant music of banged
empty cans, the violins of injured winds
in the bluegum trees guarding the fleshpots
and the scratchy groans of the *Simanje-manje*[2] bulls
charging heatedly from the grooved wax.

We held those dejected, sweat and smoke-filled
nights intimately by their elusive wasp waists
fast changing into serpents, flames
consuming the dense desire and passion thick as mist.

Here the Party's knobkerries could not reach us
under the mask of irrational and forgetful gin
and its hidden daggers, our trusted efficient weapons.
Out of those nights shall emerge
the blade of the flame that will rend the dark cloak!

1 kholoboyi   a colonial wick and can oil lamp
2 Simanje-manje   neo-modern South African township music; also called *mbaqanga*

Going Back Patiently

for Jacques-Noël Gouat

And here we are back
to the point we started from
trying to trace the path we took
but finding only traces and trails of ash
on burned down tarmac highways
showing that we too contributed
to our own destruction
letting it go on
as if it never mattered.

And if we should decide
we shall clear a new one elsewhere
in the depths of the lost primeval forest
which was facelifted and grafted
upon foreign streets for pavement
all glittering with false imitation rubies
we are back to the untimed times
and must dig and patiently too.

Then we scan the footprints of our memory
and imagination for possible clues
But violent winds have mercilessly blown
them out of our boulder-smashed minds
pell-mell into dust clouds
and laughing breezes watch us patiently digging.

Going back patiently
to starting points, eavesdropping
at keyholes to the locked past,
we are punished for window-peeping
And we must ask and ask and ask
about the hidden road that Chilembwe took,
sitting at crossroads in dilemma
watching our leaders embrace our enemies,
or starting off again on the blind road.

A Love Poem for my Country

for James

I have nothing to give you, but my anger
And the filaments of my hatred reach across the border.
You, you have sold many and me to exile.
Now shorn of precious minds, you rely only on
What hands can grow to build your crumbling image.

Your streets are littered with handcuffed men
And the drums are thuds of the warden's spiked boots.
You wriggle with agony as the terrible twins, law and order,
Call out the tune through the thick tunnels of barbed wire.

Here, week after week, the walls dissolve and are slim,
The mist is clearing and we see you naked like
A body that is straining to find itself but cannot
And our hearts are thumping with pulses of desire or fear
And our dreams are charred chapters of your history.

My country, remember I neither blinked nor went to sleep;
My country, I never let your life slide downhill
And passively watched you, like a recklessly driven car,
Hurrying to your crash, while the driver leapt out.

The days have lost their song and salt;
We feel bored without our free laughter and voice
Everyday thinking the same and discarding our hopes.
Your days are loud with clanking cuffs
On men's arms as they are led away to decay.

I know a day will come and wash away my pain
And I will emerge from the night breaking into song
Like the sun, blowing out these evil stars.

A Hanging

Zomba Central Prison

His pendulous body tolled
its own death knell from the rope
yet refused obstinately
to die, clinging desperately
to the last thread
of his condemned life.

That morning, oh!
his body sang until it could not
stand its own song;
like a guitar it hummed
and they could not but listen, stunned.
Every part of his body
opened its mouth and sang
death songs, Orphic heart songs,
shrill and sweet pent-up
songs of freedom, or sad and solemn
as the national anthem.

The heartstrings raised their harp
in a flood of insistent rhythm
and a slow drumming dance:
All his blood stood up and sang,
twisting towards the throat.
All the silent mouths raised their voices
and cried out their chorus.
No one could gag, or stop the prison
walls from singing;
No one could muzzle, or shield the ringing
echoes of Zomba mountain.
And the whispering pines on Queen's Point,
witnesses to the sordid deed,
raised their frosty mourning.

His heart was a cube of golden light,
a nest of incense where weaver-
birds had made their welcome permanent,
weaving a wall of thin silken tears
that sang with the lips of broken earth,
rolled waves, resistant and durable wind.

From every pore on his body a river of song,
or wail sprang and poured out.
His feet opened out like dark petals and chirped;
his fingers bloomed and plucked his heartstrings.
The song twined into the *makako*[1] and jammed it
the looped noose would not close, numbed.

Being political, he was not entitled
to the miraculous luck of the criminals.
So they called in the prison doctor
to administer the *coup de grace*.
He stabbed the chest with a thick
syringe and pumped the poison
into the heart with orgasmic release.

The heart made a sudden excited leap,
missed only one deceptive beat,
and resumed its journey as usual.
Slowly he turned into a deep emerald green
and covered the whole country.

Like a stone he would not die.
They summoned a hard-core life prisoner,
placed a rock hammer in his hand
and ordered him to locate the victim's heart.
He bashed in the chest completely
and left a wide yawning gap. Not murder,
technically, only routine execution.

Then a waterfall of blood! There was no one
that the blood did not touch and baptise.
Pilate searched vainly for water
to cleanse his hands of the *business*.

The song gushed out in a steady jet.
The body tolled its final knell
and then momentarily froze, then in a futile
move to cross the dark river before him,
he spread out his legs and kicked
and tried to rip the darkness that cloaked him.

Then . . . ah, this is *it*.
The final parting moment, the end, the last
wisp of breath escaping from his gaping mouth,
again with the song rising like smoke.
He wanted the last swing, the final
expression of his freedom, arrested and preserved

before the sandbags dragged his compressed body
into the dark hole, into total oblivion.

---

1 makako   the special 'crane' used for hangings in Malawian prisons

Walking Under a Tall Building

for Jacques-Noël Gouat

I carry the wet memory
of your concrete weight
on my bow-bent back
And with the long chain
of my lost friends' cadavers
I measure
your familiar intoxicating height
as you caress
the thigh of the sky.

Ah, we sent our thin voices
by steel rope and bucket
to put plaster
on your bare skeleton wall;
And we danced
to the whistle
of the overseer's whip
as it cracked
at the tongue-end
of the top boss
sucked up by your height
as we plunged deep
into the dungeons of dust,
shrunken like little ants
through the giant teeth
of the concrete mixers.

We put the glitter
in the right places
as planned and blueprinted;
Speeches, cameras, audiences,
scissors, platforms and orators
came and usurped our effort

under the dull hard thud
of the date stamps and seals
that crash close
our wailing mouths
as we scratch through
the bread lines
along the thick walls of power
where our smiles
are swindled
and our bellies groan like thunder
rolling, rumbling, chorused now
by the orders and commands
that fall from your concrete lips
down on our metal-shaven heads.

Did we erect you
to house and mother tenderly
the arrogance of secretaries
whose cosmetic voices
crackle dryly like
paper peeling
from their gory lips
and the rehearsed veneered
courtesies and
the incessant come-back-tomorrows
they fling at our faces
through the piercing screams
through their false plastic teeth
filling the quiet afternoon
drowsy streets

with the loud, uneven clatter
of writing machines
hurriedly tapped
by blood-smeared claws
their teeth trembling
in the cold Chiperoni winds;

yet, steadily, surely
churning out masses
of lies that are
stuffed down our throats, daily
like the incising insults
of the *capitao*[1] crashing,
grinding, tearing once again
through the solid spine
of my fresh memory
with the grating
of the concrete mixers
and stone cutters,
compressors and dynamite.

The long chain of insults
names you, and on your lofty face
I press my hammerprint
that will bring you crumbling down
when the day is given
when time ripens.
I am the worker, your burden
that sours your appetite,
your pillar,
the forgotten one you buried
and hid in the stuffy shanty huts,
your phantom —
Receive me back!

---

[1] *capitao*   Portuguese for captain

A Grain of Salt

I am the rock that broke apart
suddenly into so many grains only,
so many sad coarse grains,
and what I offer you now
is my most intimate grain of salt.
Between the grains tears
in gigantic globules hang
above the blood that always rises
and breaks itself into bits of sinister
laughter each a knife that wriggles
through a man's flesh and entrails
seeking his heart to plant violently
therein a poisoned tooth as wild as
the terrible seed that sprouts
all over Malawi today, dark as hatred.
The knife and flesh twist helplessly about:
The knife without a will of its own
and the man taken by total
surprise killed by surprise too
and his grains of salt scattered
among the bitter nights of March,
the knife waving desperately
like a severed tongue whose native
language tastes of blood, ash and salt;
and the blade tastes flesh
relishing it before it buries itself
in the crotch and goes to sleep there forever.
The tongues of the giant flames lick huts
in which this exhausted salt rests
charring it till its scream is stifled
And everywhere in the country desolate shells
of huts touched by this terrible heat indict,
everywhere a fire like opened flowers blossoms
and everything is swallowed in its stomach.
A legion of coarse grain salt plagues prisoners;

it has invaded all the prisons, detention camps
and concentration centres, and raised its voice.
It is hard lead in their six-hour-old porridge
and in their red beans it tastes like a bitter verdict:
There it weeps forlornly behind the smoke;
It had died here and left its weight in the chains.

The grain that slipped through the long fingers
of the combing rake, I am that salt;
Torrential sweat and blood sticky
with salt pour from me carelessly.
You want me to be more specific?
This and this and this and this:
A giant grain of salt and an enormous
bead of sweat sit on the face of the capital
city tortured but shining brightly:
The rands and the immense sweat meet here
and the money insolently barks its orders
and the men swarm about with burdens like ants:
They are lugging the bundles of salt that fell
because salt is never certain where next
it will fall. A man brought rotten rands
coated in salt and deposited them here,
the snare perfectly concealed from the man
who, unsuspecting, took the money
and left his only heart here, trapped.
Look at all that salt hooded,
blindfolded in a dark sisal sack;
the sun sitting astride the broken man
and the wails of salt crashing through
the iron prison roof like one huge arrow
because the whole country is a vast prison
and all the salt is trembling in the cold
July winds in nothing but tattered sacks.
The heavy echoes of the salt's sobs
thunder through the crystal waves:
It has sweated all over the sad soil

and rained on the tortured waters.
My little grain sings the same song
and everyone who listens weeps uncontrollably.

Sometimes the body is willing
to break itself into so many minute parts
and give itself wholly to its native land.
But let it decide on its own, for
at times the body wishes for integrity
especially if it is, like man, a lump of salt.
Today I am that grain of salt
that is both bitter and sweet,
And I want to return to the days I joined men
house to house, hand to hand, unrepulsed;
I want to be present all over the earth
and simultaneously remain in my country.
I have stood in the lions' den
and overpowered them with my salt's song,
and all those praised fierce lions
it is here they must come to be tamed.

I have kept everything mine
crossed:
fingers crossed, everything
every Sunday crossed, my heart crossed
till my skin has worn off the knees
of my soul hoping that my most intimate grain
of salt will return like a ship
presumed lost in a high storm.
I touch everything with this ferocious salt
in love and then in hate, for I am
the sun that screamed through the male rain
and gave an intense rainbow to our country.
Remember, I am the rock that broke apart
suddenly into many shining grains
and what I offer you is my most intimate grain of salt
And its sweet song still haunts our land.

The Dark Veil

for Jack Mapanje

Poet, if you come in the rain, in a forgotten season,
The dark veil that grips our country
Will greet you with its ruthless sword.
The chill abroad sharpened your anger;
The cold gluttonous hearts fired and honed your love;
Grasp her tenderly by her wasp waist,
Yank the veil off her sparkling ruby eye,
And peer deeply at your image in the crystal lake:
Recover and reclaim your stolen smile, and
The fresh laughter of your tuned guitar.

New Haven, CT: 5 December 1981

Singing Like Parrots

for Ngũgĩ wa Thiong'o

'*I call on all ministers, assistant ministers and every other person to* sing like parrots.'
An African Head of State

And so the mind, emptied, rots
into a parrotry of sing-song praises:
You dance to the rattle of your chains
— on your arms, on your legs —
You wail from lips split by constant whips
Necklaces of your tears adorn your necks.
You have pawned your lives for the right
to sing in the beak of a hawk. Your
Disciplined thighs sigh open
and dish out rewards
to murderers, firm-beaked cocks
with fire crested on their heads
poke and poke and poke at
the *Loyal* forbidden fruit whose juice
leaks into the toxic Kachasu gin
and the Carlsberg beer that turns their heads.
Obedient breasts unleash a torrent
of milk and bittersweet honey
that drown the country under floods of songs.
And they sing like parrots while envious men
fondle their thoughts like rosary beads, afraid
to breach the false *Unity,* while
the sour cassava of poisoned slogans
brews a whirlwind in the earthen vessel.
Ministerial mouths perpetually open,
swallow the morsels of power that drop
from the peak of the paternal beak.
Inflamed, they sing like parrots also
Praises to the impotent wolf-faced hawk
with talons dipped in our blood.

16 September 1984

Again, the Dagger Speaks

Upon hearing about the new wave of killings

Eloquent in the terrible tongue of terror,
the dagger stutters in the language of peace.
Only corpses and skeletons laugh at its jokes
as they roll in the dust, headless and dying of laughter
laced with the sad blood of Mikuyu Detention Centre;
The blood flaps on the tricoloured flag
that lashes us all with the icy whips of Chiperoni winds
its razor-edge slicing our necks like a guillotine.
The dagger had tattooed the doors of peace
and its terrible tongue wags in the hand of the noble tyrant.
The dagger with the mirrored blade where the curious get cut,
It lured our flowers and chopped them down;
Yet among the bamboo groves the noble tongues of spears
Recently descended from the sooty rafters
Hum a new song of freedom, a song without blood.
But the dagger is still talkative amid the deafening silence
As it shaves our villages clean of the new grass
And we scurry into our heated holes like scared rats,
Into the tiny Chingwe's Holes to suffocate on silence,
On a starvation ration of sponsored ignorance.
But the spear forged in the heat of struggle,
Locked in the arsenal of freedom, breaks loose
And sows a seed of lightning to clean out the dirt.
Emperors tremble at their own shadows and entomb themselves,
The martyr-makers with a chaos of corpses at their feet,
Clutch their hearts under the mangoes' hard tears.

The Emperors for Life

Dash out of history's footnotes
Armed with titles, medals and pen-pistols,
Knee-deep in perennial pools of blood,
Ride in hammocked on broken backs,
And land into giant thrones of polished bones.

Every Sunday afternoon, in Africa,
The emperors for life wearing garlands
Of dry human bones, stroll through their palatial
Gardens of wailing flowers and bleeding brooks
Sipping a rare Bordeaux of chilled plasma

Like palm wine tapped from their lands' hearts.
At nightfall, they dine on choice leg *bonne femme*
From imperial fridges, stewed intestines filled
With diamonds pilfered from the commonweal
And nuggets from the custom-made thrones.

Official Papa smiles grace the People's Palaces
Etched in dementia, ringed with crimson
As they snuff life in the bud and wallow in comfort
On behalf of the people, on the shoulders of the land.

October 1986

The Bitter Onions

Something as old as hate, sweet
and bitter as love, snuggles
in the belly of the onion
who puffs himself up like an angry toad,
loading all his fury into his flimsy
silken coat where unfathomable depths
and sadnesses reside, in the mirrors
of its bitter sap that scalds
the treacherous messianic dolts,
the aristocratic grasshoppers,
the sap that, like a scorpion
with fire in its tail, stings and
stings the gluttonous urchins seated
on the dungheap of our embezzled dreams.
The furious sap of the bitter onions
burns the hands that try to pickle
them in the pepper of hatred,
in the oil of pain, over a brutal fire
of Independence, burns through
the gullet and builds a thorny nest
in the swollen tearbud of the tyrant.

I will not mention the fallen;
Funerals are banned, censored today.
In Blantyre you died among the fish
Everywhere roasted, baked among the penned cattle,
Denied peace, sizzling in the Gehenna.
Behind the wire, on the angry soil, on
the tortured, insulted mountain peaks,
Only the bitter onions refused to sing praises!
Obstinate fruit, tuber ever succulent:
you grow, you grow round surreptitiously
udder filled with underground milk:
There is no poetry to equal your tear, your rain.
A grain of earth, a taste of soil clings
to your gnarled, withered leaf.

Onions heaped on the funeral pyre, ready for martyrdom,
The unspeakable fires you have bathed in
Drinking the bitter wine of the earth,
Buried in mass unmarked graves, in green rivers
Left for dead: yet —
You sprouted and sent forth
rays of a rare sun;
When they tear you out of your soil,
your minute seed will go on germinating
hiding your courage under
each layer of your scarred lives.

The Birds of State

Our fat national roosters drag their pot-bellies
like an epidemic of chronic pregnancies
As they chew on the generous chunky crumbs of a cake
baked in a foreign oven, proferred to us as aid.
We shower praises on their snowy crunching teeth
As they burn us out with the terrible fire
They carry proudly on their dunder heads.
We shower praises as they tread our patriotic hens,
Their cheeks like *Chitute*[1] rats after a harvest
from our half-full granaries left unprotected
As we drink distilled sweat and fermented urine
And feast on the blood-filled fleas that suck us
Between our shoeless toes and gulleys in our soles.
We shower praises on these national cocks perched on
The daughters of the nation shunted from rally to rally
Polishing the long black cars with their sweet songs.
Swollen-bellied, dark-feathered, they cavort on the lofty
Dunghills where the national bulls have defecated
And shower us with their profuse urine of slogans,
Open their wings and clap us with a fatal thunder
As we polish their dark feathers with more praise songs.

23 March 1990

---

[1] *Chitute* the ugly mouse that amasses food

In the House of Power

*Flowers labour
in the house of power.*
Pestilence and tyranny
cheer them on:

Between the anvil
and the iron hammer:
*Flowers labour
in the house of power*

Between the cudgel
and the pen-pistol:
*Flowers labour
in the house of power*

Under the concrete
of Plantation House:
*Flowers labour
in the house of power*

In the sweat and blood
of the tortured labourer:
*Flowers labour
in the house of power*

Under the dead weight
of national monuments:
*Flowers labour
in the house of power*

Under the gaze
of the epicene eyes:
*Flowers labour
in the house of power*

In the veneer
of old Victorian desks:
Flowers labour
in the house of power

Between heaven, hell
and the incinerator:
Flowers labour
in the house of power

Clipped phalluses
and perforated wombs:
Flowers labour
in the house of power

Flowers labour
in the house of power
fanning a flame
sharpening a spear.

Pot Bellies and Swollen Cheeks

Mene, mene, tekel, upharsin
Thou art weighed in the balance and found wanting

Double-chinned worms, humongous as hippos,
necks drowned in mountainous fat, drag
pot bellies like chronic pregnancies,
grinding mills working in their tireless mouths
as they chew on the lean national cake
baked in a foreign overseas oven
and coated in a chilly sugar of aid.
We shower them with praises as their snowy teeth
churn our land and bury it in their bellies.
We bless them with our cleansing saliva
as they burn us with the blazing cocks-
combs on their heads, their cheeks like bellows.
We fatten these worms on half-full granaries,
while we drink distilled sweat, our fermented urine,
and feast on blood-filled fleas that suck us dry
in the tiny dark cells where they pen us.
Wherever they fart, victims fall headlong
into ditches, swallow dust and chew a handful of earth
red as their own blood siphoned out of their necks
while the worms crawl up the sweet thighs of the
paw-paw breasted daughters of the nation
polishing the long black cars with praise songs.

23 March 1990

My Aunt's Tales

In my aunt's tales,
Eagle-headed women
marry half birds, half men;
One-legged women swarm the night,
Kiss one-legged leprous men
And make them whole again.

I surrender myself to the tales,
in the dream, by the folkloric riverside,
dress the leprous woman's wounds,
and get a handful of blessings
from her gnarled fingers.

Suddenly, I am the hawk-headed man
Hot after the tigress woman
who sinks her sharp claw into my neck
in the heat of the moment

And the tales swallow me.
From dream to dream I rise
Light blossoming from my palms,
I rise through exile, to dawn
I swim through the dark river
As the night swallows her again.

Matiningale

from a Malawian folk-tale

Though you fell for
a monkey in a three-piece suit,
and sank a few thorns
in my palms when last I held you,
luminous flower,
wasp-waisted stem with secret
tattoos that I stroked
on your dark, silken thighs,
beheaded flowers festering at your feet,
my affair with you
has not ended, though
with your fangs
you greeted the kiss
I planted on your mouth,
and the *ants* gnaw
the crystals of light
from my hand
that stirred your sweet water,
though your special *bees*
feast on my fingers of silence,
though you have succumbed,
my love, to the hard caresses
of the devils
who finger your secret waist beads
and fondle the grains
of your hidden millet;
our affair is not over,
though you throttle the doves
that once cooed in your throat
not over yet,
though gaunt hoarse voices
rage through your sweet mouth
ravaged by the punch

of the subtle *Uchema*[1] wine
dripping from the split nape
of the beheaded palm tree,
as you labour under
impotent despots
while your suitors
plunge, one by one,
into the dungeons,
or innumerable Chingwe's Holes
and you fall and fall and fall,
Matiningale, harsh beautiful land,
I will never abandon you,
flower of light, light of my heart.

5 October 1988

---

[1] *Uchema*   Nyanja for palm wine

The Singing Drum

for Nabanda

from a Nyanja folk-tale

Your sweet voice is trapped in the drum
That sings praises to a gelded lion
Whose magic tail lured you back to the river
Where his wide-mouthed drum awaited your voice.
He put out his claws, caressed you lovingly
As you searched for your lost waist beads,
And tamed you into his hoarse drum.
Now he bleeds you for his coffers amid drunken
Orgies: between your fat haunches flow coerced
Gifts: fourteen thousand eggs, a century of goats,
You dance out innumerable chickens, granaries
Of maize, flocks of sheep ooze out as you wail
Sweetly from feast to feast to feats of false
Heroics and histrionics in a hail of slogans.
You sing out a million Kwacha at a time
Into the Swiss banks, as your accordion-ribbed
babies shrivel and shrink at your ample nipples.
Sister, your sweet voice wails in a foreign drum.

15 June 1990

III
THE STRANGE GRAVES

I don't want to be a poet anymore,
the heroes are under the ground
the games are over.
Miodrag Pavlovich

The Killing Grounds

I am talking about villages
that disappeared
without leaving orphans
wiped off the maps
just like that!
pagan villages
offensive to Christian eyes,
villages that reeked the smell
of elephant meat
on a three-stone hearth,
villages that carried
on their heads
the noble names
of ancient African kings
and warrior queens:
These are what I am
talking about,
villages that went
peacefully to sleep one night
and never woke up
again,
where the cocks
never crowed three times
at the hour of betrayal
because a tongue of fire
had licked them to death
the way the predatory python
cheats his prey;
villages that never fought

but with fragile arrows
or bows that sang of love,
villages without knowledge
of mines, bombs or bazookas,
villages that for centuries

had snuggled against the belly
of a river called The Father of Peace
where nights writhed with dance
and trembled with song,
where people made love
and stored it in their hearts
for the lean seasons,
villages where, like Adam and Eve,
people dressed formally
in fig leaves
and threw care to the winds,
and erect spears hunted everywhere
and nothing was done in secret.
But stealthily, one December night,
white hawks
spewed the hot shit of lead
on those villages with names
like surnames of peace-loving
people freely giving
and receiving love
in those tropical nights.
Those were the villages
the Christian men,
drunk on the wine of hatred,
erased with the flame of prejudice,
villages whose summer buds
and tender sprouts
they chopped with shrapnel.
Ah, the sons of Europe
and their fine deeds,
who handcuffed babies
with their own intestines,
and trimmed their mothers' tender arms
with swords of steel crosses:
Wiriyamu, Chimoio, Nhazonia,
Cassinga, Chikumbi, Feira,
villages that made their way

painfully into history
but stayed in the shadows
because flowers exuded
more fragrant songs
than sizzling flesh.
And when the Christian boys left,
they took away the barks,
the bleats, the neighs, the meows,
and appointed silence
to reign in their absence
amid the stilled pestles
that had once moved lovingly
in the receptive mortars.
The villages now erased
from our memories,
these are what you and I
shall talk about
a million years hence,
the villages
that disappeared
from the face of the earth
without a trace
because they were buried
in unmarked trenches.

September 1978

Wiriyamu

for Adrian Hastings, lest we forget

A demented thoroughbred bull
with salazar's eyes
and caetano's fangs
burst out
of the halls of justice
drunk on communion wine,
balancing hatred on its horns, and
raged across the Sahara,
through the sad tropics,
till it blindly stopped at Wiriyamu.
From its enormous phallus
it spewed a swarm
of little freckle-faced salazars
and caetanos sunburnt like us,
almost men, almost children,
reckless and elated on their first kaffir hunt,
their rite of passage,
as they clutched barrels
loaded with hatred and fear
left over from Beira and Mueda
wielding blazing crosses
that sowed corpses in the cassava mounds.
Over the make-shift butcher blocks,
the drunken *soldados¹* pruned
our pagan children,
opened wombs and tortured
tiny guerrilla fetuses, and
caroused on their mothers' blood.
'Exterminate the Natives', cried Chiko,
their black Lusophone parrot,
in His Master's Voice,
the faithful servant of the Empire
cheered his little masters

in their gruesome duty.
The *soldados*, photogenic
with their trusted automatics,
brandished bouquets of wrenched
limbs and uprooted genitals,
ribs barbequed over angry charcoal,
to be washed down with cheap
Eusebio wine.
Fired up,
they sprayed the hot
hard shit of carnivorous lead
on the village slumbering
in its defiant dreams.
The crosses blazed the night into day,
the stubborn earth
into a bubbly porridge
that scalded the tongue
of the great Zambezi
as it licked and cooled
the scorched earth
like a goat its newborn,
licked the blood off the land,
cleansed the women impaled
on the sharpened crosses,
the babies draped over
the silent and vigilant baobabs,
the fetuses interrogated by bayonets.
And the children peeled their lips
and laughed at the bull
spewing larva on the children
who split their lips and
ha! ha! ha! and peeled their eyes
and stared the bull into a thicket
of darkness where it cowered and
opened its mouth and vomited
napalm on the defenceless
children who curled their lips

and died laughing, while
booby-trapped babies
brained against the pregnant
baobabs, wrung up like laundry,
unleashed their boiling laughter,
girls raped with muzzles,
crucified grandmothers, emaciated men
chopped up and tossed in a crazy salad,
in the earthen bowl of a yawning trench,
let out one loud guffaw and shup up again,
their mutilated bodies
searching for their heads
by the light blazing from their hands.
And thus the war dragged its belly
all over Mozambique, rousing
the elephants of anger, the dormant lions,
furious and passionate doves
that cooed the heavy secret, aroused
the enraged drums that sang
through the fuming bowstrings
till Gungunyana's and Maguiguana's
living spears descended from the rafters
and gyrated over the ravaged crosses
left by the fleeing soldados.
And peace draped Wiriyamu like a dew.

---

[1] *Soldados* Portuguese for soldiers

Nhazonia

Nhazonia, come out of that rat hole
where they buried you,
where your wounds sob
in the dark angry night.
They will not strangle the rainbow,
or snuff out the dawn
that is as certain as a rainbow
in a male rain.
A blood-stained rainbow
arches across the puddles
of a rain made in Lisbon.
Between your huge legs,
a mass grave swallows
the four hundred innocents.
With sharp chain saws they
mash up the bodies
into ground beef, *Fray Bentos*
sausages, or cheap *sostis*[1]
bound for the metropole.
Out of the ash, Nhazonia, rise
rise again like a great bird
and soar again over
Cahora Bassa, over the Zambezi.
We shall sew back onto your trunk,
your dismembered limbs
hacked with axes.
Nhazonia, Nhazonia,
my arrow pierces the dirty clouds;
They peel apart like a fruit coat,
and sunlight streams down
like sweet juice,
and my rainbow
reappears across the sky.
Nhazonia, come back home.

---

1 sostis   a corruption of 'sausages' in the speech of ex-miners returning from South Africa

Shrapnel

Your name is stuck
on a dangerous weapon:
sharp stainless steel name,
almost a shark, with cruel jaws.
They are perfecting its pitiless
blades in Nicaragua and El Salvador;
They whetted them in Vietnam
where they defoliated people
with the harsh consonants
and heartless vowels of your name.
How could you hate people
so much you sought an efficient
arm to wipe them off the earth?
They have inherited your
callous hands and are putting up war
for sale all over the world.

Ah, Shrapnel, I know one day your name
was sweet in the mouth of your lover:
Now it rhymes with scrap metal,
the death knell and all that is lethal.
You stand between people and chop off
their hands before their greetings,
their faces frowning with jaws of shrapnels
below their murderous, pepper-red eyes.
Like a worm you have stealthily
entered national budgets and bulged them.
Like a mouse, you chew on the heart of the world
and breathe an intoxicating breath on it.
You marched madly through Mozambique, Angola,
Guinea Bissau, Zimbabwe. Like a whirlwind
you are dancing drunkenly in Northern Ireland today
pruning young children and putting stumps
on their shoulders and arms.
With your accomplices, Sam and Grenade,

You are wreaking havoc today in the Middle East.
You are presiding at the butcher conferences
You are sharing out the assorted meats at the banquets.

Yet, these I wish to know:
Did you have a child, a wife who awaited
your tender caresses and wild love-making?
Let History tell me how tender your touch was.
Did your hand ever plant a tree?
Today, your name is
the name of a lethal weapon.
Today, your name is hatred.

The Burning Rose

an elegy for Mkwapatira Mhango

You handed them a rose of truth
but they pitched it in the fire

The rose burst into *Lux in Tenebris* and raged
across the early morning lake
from Mulowe to Monkey Bay
And the rose rose and bled and fell down,
rose and bled, rose and bled, and flew
up in one raging flame that licked your house,
and ate up your wives, swallowed your children
and your guests like a rose hungry for love;
And the rose flapped against the walls
of the house that rose in flames like fiery roses;
And the rose bared its thorns in a lovely snarl,
Thorns hefty like a crazed cow's goring horns,
Hoofed with hatred, while a blazing petal
Wagged its long tongue up through the roof
And licked the children's cries
that rang like cathedral bells clanging
in the bald-headed tyrant's ears. And the rose,
Kyrie Eleison, fell like showers of clotted
blood poured in lavish libations on the kerosene
rose that bloomed from a terrible match stick.

3 January 1990

Madonnas and Children

for Ethiopian and Sudanese Refugees

Maize-stalk babies
open palms
like withered petals
bloomed prematurely
from stone-hard bellies
where hunger rages
and intestines chew
on their own membrane walls
and weave cocoon balls
of biting hunger.
Their mothers' breasts,
pale shrunken flaps
stuck to their chests,
above the accordion ribs,
are elephant ears
that swell under the bite
of the babies' brittle lips
leeched to dry nipples
as the tiny ghosts suck
their mothers' spent lives
through the deflated bosoms
and drain the overflowing
wells of pain.
In the close-up shot
on this special 'African Journey',
the bloated bellies bud out
through the screen
at the obese woman whose disposable
baby swirls down the toilet
as she smothers the fire
that the scorching soaps
have lit between her haunches.
The tattered skeletal

scarecrows' bones puncture
their drum hides and blossom
through the screen
into a corolla
of dented enamel begging bowls.

Death drops relief into them:
A penny for the old scarecrows;
A hepenny for the blind Madonnas.

The Orphan Boy of Kampala

he could not find
in any human tongue
words for mankind,
mankind who live on.
    Czeslaw Milosz

A fabled child sits on the seventh hill
marooned in a sea of polished skulls;
He cannot look a man in the face;
He has turned his back on the human race.
He says, the human face appals him;
In a smile he sees an insane snarl.
He will not return to the human race.
Though mute, salvaged from the monkeys,
He hears the mockery in his dying father's laughter.
He says he has found humanity in a dog:
His belly bulges with salty clay and grass
garnered from his daily grazing among cattle.
A bitter seed sprouts from his belly,
The same seed that burst Uganda at the seams;
It shoots for his heart and his dead emotions
Where a mocking bird has planted its teary laughter
And a python has caressed him with its fangs:
His silent song, *Let us go to Lowero*
Where my father was killed
That we may kill them all with my elephant gun,
has eaten out his human heart among the sprouting skulls.

Soweto Child

a poem for children

As the silvery moon softly crawls silently into the sky
And I slip out to play night games with my friends,
I hear the wind weeping in the distance, over Soweto;
A child like me, his breath cut short by bullets,
Dangles lifelessly from his mother's warm tender arms;
A smile mixed with blood gently parts his mouth.
Fear shoots his sharp arrows down my spine,
But the round smiling moon sings softly to me:

Child, sow your blood, Soweto child, feed your people with fire
Flaming high, stand up and let it lick you clean:
You are the new promise of the future for your people.

Soweto is us children flaming through the chains, breaking them;
The pride of our mothers as we tear the boots from our mouths;
So let us dance with spears and shields and laugh with the moon.

Remembering Soweto: 1978

Initially I was tempted to name "Hector Pieterson"(12) as the first child to be shot down on June 16, 1976 during the Soweto Uprising. New information has surfaced suggesting that the first such child was "Hastings Ndlovu" (15). I want to name those children, but how many names will I need to identify all those children who lie in the mass graves of Central and Southern Africa! What to do?

IV
ATLANTIC CROSSING

◊

Exile is round in shape,
a circle, a ring.
Your feet go in circles, you cross land
and it's not your land.
Light wakes you up and it's not your light.
Night comes down, but your stars are missing.
You discover brothers, but they're not of your blood.
Pablo Neruda

Atlantic Crossing

for Lawrence F. Sykes

*O sea, are you the sea
that no one crosses?*
from an Ijaw tale, Nigeria

The huge American jet runs like a madman
along the London tarmac, European dust stuck
to its eagle claws, and suddenly bounds for the sky
in a mock giant leap for mankind
wrenching itself free of the English soil.

Seated slave-ship pattern, we arrow
supersonically for the calm pocket of Congo air.
Suspended, tossing here and there for centuries,
we watch the subtle smoke settle
like a mother hen over her eggs
over the old sagging English island and channel
her dreams of heroic pirates and greatness unhatched.

As we conquer the vast sea-sky
I lower a large tombstone into the depths:
a rough stone with life dates of my ancestors
sunken naked, stripped of their names.

On the screens, for a buck and quarter, America
reaches out her *strange fruit* hung from a rope
from an oak tree straining against its weight
under it salivating wolves bare their teeth.

Below us, as New England villages unravel
from the mist like old postcards,
Plymouth Rock secretly fingers our muscles
with her sharp nickle nails.

Amid millions of blinking eyes that explode
from immense towers of glass, steel and concrete,
I land on the worn out auction block
with two prices on my head. *Lady Liberty,* with
false eye-lashes and eye-shadow, lures me
into her cold hard embrace, monstrous lights
popping out of her head crowned with a withered sun.

She tosses me onto her unbalanced scale:
My soul, weighed against her old sin, tips over
to the right as figures encircle my head;
famished foxes scramble for my exotic muscle.

Twice I call her: New York, New York:
Insatiable prostitute, her ears blocked
with southern cotton and northern snow.
She smashes my heart across Wall Street
paved with mosaics of slave hides and whale bone:

In her windowed head rages hell fire
in her torch where men are daily roasted
like Kentucky fried chicken and hamburgers!

Farewell Street

And before I be a slave
I will be buried in my grave
And go home to my Lawd and be free
           from a spiritual

In Farewell Street you shed your serf's
skin, your neck iron, cuffs, manacles
as you descend from your cross and mount
the ladder of bones from your dead kinsmen
that rises before you to your African heaven.
As you ready for your final flight home,
you glance last at this frigid land;
From your wishes sprout two wings
that will bear you across the Atlantic;
Your mistress's tears won't ransom you
from death's sweet song that seduces you
across the humped waves, the lonely nauticals —
Homeward bound, you smile Brer Rabbit's smile
as you take your last turn into God's Acre
for a brief repose. You lift your soul
and wave it like a handkerchief, whisking
away servitude and the plantation, though
Zango Stevens' sculptured stone presses
on the dreams of freedom in your kinky head.
Your wings spread out finally as home looms . . .
Farewell, fly well, dishonoured guest, fly away
Home.

Upon visiting God's Acre, Newport, RI: August 1980

God's Acre

for Barbara and Larry

Your Datsun battered like an ancestor
on the Providence Plantations
genuflects gently towards ancestral dust
kept under slate slabs and sculptured headstones
in segregated God's Acre.
Cemented with mortar mixed with that head-
spinning rum from Rumford, Rhode Island,
some bitter history lies submerged, silent,
in this vandalised slaveyard sunken
with Kedindo, Cape Coast James
and Zango Stevens whose deft fingers
left his stamp in the signatures
in the silent stones over the urn of African dust
strewn on this hostile soil many moon-
miles away from the old country.
You lay the bones to rest again, this treasure-
trove of historied clay pirated in hatches.
You fondle this ancestral loam, this *juju*
that harbours your names, centuries squeezed
into a few grains of sand, and reach your probosis
into the dark and bloody centuries
to rescue our plundered history. As your shutter
clicks tirelessly, our face emerges again
on bromide solarised out of this piece
of American sod, out of God's Acre.

Newport, RI: August 1980

This Island Now

for René Belance

A blade borrows its blue
face from the moon,
an orange face from the fire,
and multiplies its epidemic
of hideous stars
with red angry eyes:

Steel blade in this vestibule
of terrible air,
its monstrous stare
trained on your sensuous mouth
as it glares night and day
with bared unblinking eyes
above the smarting wounds
in the scorching sun
fuelled by the flaming waves.

Above you, dark clouds deafened
by harsh loud jetsongs sharpen
the lip of the steel blade, above
the citadel it wields its hatred
of dark skin and bargains for time:
with its subtle starry eyes
and a devilish blue wink
it bares its monstrous snarl:

It creeps cowboy fashion
down the marble stairways
quietly, quietly approaches,
stealthily readies for the ambush:
the fatal plunge between your ribs
into your coveted flesh:

Wails of sea-buried bones in centuries
of voodoo songs rise out of the waves
clenching their anger against the claw.

Island with a sad broken back,
scarred and mutilated face,
bobbing belly-up like a giant fish
speared by a reckless urchin's hand
completely drained of your furious Arawak gold,

In your wounds the pulse of the earth
murmurs Toussaint's word into the sky
with the tremor of forgotten water,
the pale hungry ocean whitened
by alien foam and waste water.
Island twice deflowered by strange
lecherous harpoons and iron petals
A giant chandelier of tears leaps
out of your sacred stone and prepares to flame.

Wizard

for Sterling A. Brown, on your birthday

Your hammer prints its arc on the face
of the sky when you swing
A thousand birds in your rock hammer
suck the moist sky and sing an intense song
swollen like a wounded heart.

Your ten pound hammer plucks the sun
which you hammer till it showers its southern
warmth all over the earth.
Under your hammerblows we shed the blinding
fish scales and see the rivers in the rainbow

the rainbows and whirlwinds in a teardrop:
You beat the sweat into a jewel,
the broken chain link into a diamond
rare as the sea star, and hammer
the diamond into a rainbow whose
translucent crystal hangs down your furrowed face:

The ring of John Henry's hammer in your mouth
And its dazzling rainbow in your eyes,
Your hammerblow cracks and wounds the rock:
Pure water jets out of it. You are the sun
That pierces the dewdrop: your rainbow hugs your land:

When you talk into the steel, the steel sings;
When you speak into the rock, the rock cries out
And the restless water in your mouth hums,
Rears like the Mississippi, thunders like the wild Atlantic.

When you look into the iron, the iron flares
into the embittered cane singing in the wind:
Your arms are railroad tracks that embrace

the land you know like a lover's body
whose sap drums through your toughened veins
its pulses and your hammerblows singing through your blood.

Yes, you will die with your talking hammer in your hand.

New Haven: 1 May 1981

Night Exodus

The footfalls of those who
Vanished in the dark thunderstorms
Ring towards my dimly-lit room;
Advancing shadows ducking searchlights,
Their voices cracked and broken:
A bloody blur fading into night, echoes
Leave behind silhouettes
Of nightmares, abandoned mutilated hopes. Behind,
They shower sad, beaten flowers, scarred
Broken men, spirits whipped and tortured,
Chains exerting their grip
On their necks, stifling each forming word.
The shadow behind each life
Lingers after the life itself has been snuffed.
The dark rain curtains off those in exodus.

In Exile

Your heart lifts its wings
when the grass knows your touch,
the great ladders of rain beat tattoos,
the thunder roars like a million lions,
And the eyes of your heart smile
when the stale rain brings you an aroma
of mangoes in the faded news.
Your teeth question each shrimp
and scorpion of the sea when
America burns your mouth.
In nightmares you search for the angelic
babies in your people's satanic faces.
In the cacophony of foreign voices
which are sort of kind of like free
for all, you polish your own, plane
your tongue and fight to guard
your children's tongues from tres-
passing on the unkempt lawn
of this chaotic language. Your face
is missing from those that rise to greet you.
A word that recently fell into your mother tongue
arrives stutteringly late to tell the joke,
unable to name the plants smiling in your garden.
Like a goat in heat, you sniff the air
for the familiar scent of *Chikasu*.[1]
The sun walks crazily far away from you
And in summer, gives you more shine
than you can use when it takes ages to set.
And in the winter it sulks and hands you
a lump of darkness to last a century.
You scour the sky for the white bow-tied crows
And every so often you pick up your shell,
Crawl to more safety, your toes always pointing homewards.
When you utter the name of your country,
everybody knows you are a Martian
and scurries for the most latest map.

11 June 1990

[1]*Chikasu* Nyanja for curry

Ukimbizi

Humiliation opens every door,
greets you with fingers of icicles
and bids you farewell before
your feet have touched her feet.
Exile steps in and strips you
of your royal skin and
you grovel as a beggar.
She seizes you by your bamboo hair
and pitches you out through the window
into the street that waits to swallow you
like a famished shark while
the air outside embraces you
with its porcupine prickles
that sink down to strangle
your frail heartstrings.
No wonder you cherish the true
friends who become your kin
and take you into their blood.
In their hearts you glimpse
the bright stars of home again,
and in their sweet laughter
you hear your own rich waves.

Northfield: 11 June 1990

Ode to a Congo Pygmy in the Bronx Zoo

Ota Benga (c.1881 – 1916)

I watch you from this side of pain:
Barricaded as a bear, or circus lion,
caged on the plantation, chain for neck-
lace, yoked ever to the plough,
you rage from steel bar to steel bar,
your banana-hardened teeth break on the bar,
beating your chest, threatening your captors:
I watch you from this unsafe bank of history,
strapped in my own invisible cage
whose bars criss-cross in the temple of my mind.
Will you please be black and beautiful
for the tourist cameras that salivate
at your flopping oversized forbidden fruit
that would earn you a rope and a swing
from Governor Lynch were you let loose.

Brother, calm down and wrap yourself
in your bars. You are an endangered species.

Toronto: April 1990

Requiem for an African Woman in a Glass Case in Paris

Saartjie Baartman (1789-1816)

An African woman stands naked in a glass case
where she finds no rest from the circuses and fairs,
Stands guard over the mores of the Western world.
No mystery here; hers is an eternal striptease:
Her forbidden mango bared and exhibited
in the Museum of Man as an oddity of nature.
In 1814 she took Paris by storm, grabbed her
by the neck, and squeezed the Eiffel steel out.
Like a witch she blazed out her secret lamp
and Europe crowded round her glass hut.
France, salivating like a hungry wolf, flocked
to ogle at her bulbous buttocks and pendulous breasts,
the flaps she could not cover with her palms,
his long chameleon tongue licking the glass case.
At the sumptuous banquets, men tamed their lust
on her barbequed thighs and decanted brains
that went to waste on their antique china,
and calmed their gluttonous scramble
with the sweet fermented wine and palm oil
from her mysterious secret delta. Gutted
with brandy and lewd words that poisoned her heart,
she has stood there for a century, Hottentot Venus, staring
at men's folly, debased and spineless, in her glass prison.

16 June 1990

Ms. Baartman's body arrived in Cape Town, South Africa, on Friday, May 3, 2002, in a coffin draped in the South African flag, and was finally properly interred in her homeland on August 9, 2002.

Ebony Root

Iron-eyed vultures
have muffled the soft sigh
of cowhide drums in the piercing
squeal of butchered doves

at the deep end
of the blinding night
through the hawks' claws
submerged in blood pools.

The root had to die
 to live in this face.

The men are dried tree trunks
on termite hills where
politicians drunk
on power and the embezzled
commonweal, dance, reeling.

The men are dried tree trunks:
gnawed, gaunt, on the termite hill.

The sobs, the smiles on empty
bellies, the snarls —
all are frozen in this face
that stares at me darkly.

In these wide eyes
the drummed rhythm of the vendor's
chant at the Livingstone
roadside tourist market, rings:

Ebeni wood, best wood
Ebeni wood, pure wood
Ebeni wood, dark wood
Ebeni wood, real root

Beneath the song rings
A chorus of detainee's cries
As they ride the terrible horse
And the wood takes root
up their broken spines.

Providence, RI: 1978

Tikambepo

unmailable letter to Jack Mapanje
(I know this poem will not unlock the prison gate)

and our greatest
hope
will be to find out
next year
that they're still torturing him
eight months later
Ariel Dorfman

Today the devil bird lays
your hard-boiled brain
in a barbed-wire nest
where your manacled thoughts
moulder behind concrete
walls and steel bars,
you who went to tune your crude
bangwe[1] in a cold foreign land
and returned home where dogs
sniffed your footprints
for dissent, listening
for secret pulses of revolt
in your secret arteries where
lust and erotic blood burned
for your lover, your land
naked before you.
With a cudgel they try to extract
a speck from your keen eye
that saw the specks in theirs!
Ah! brother, we must go to school
again about life, I know:
They misunderstood you when you
called for Mercy, you called for your wife,
And Courage you called your daughter.
And Courage we call to your side.

15 November 1988

[1] *bangwe* thumb piano

A Crane from Home

after Gervog Emin

I know you come from home, dear crane,
Bearing a bright coal of pain between your beak,
Your wings straining against your bright chains,
Your eyes squinting through the blinders.

Let me tap the ash off your wings, dear crane,
Straighten your feathers and fill them with flight.
Perch on the extended twig of my arm, snap your chains,
Flap your wings again, and pour forth your free song.

Let me soothe your eyes, mend your broken ribs,
Dear crane, heal your scars, dry your tears and give you
A place for rest, a nest to nurse your wounded heart,
Not a prison house, new chains and a new pain.

A hundred thousand welcomes, dear crane,
From the land where tyrants father born-again Christians,
The land of detentions, assassinations and poisonings,
Where live or dead secrets hide in car trunks.

Where you come from, dear crane,
Merciless lions and foxes hunt helpless rabbits,
Shroud the secret murders in the dark dark veils,
And muffle subversive wails of bereaved mothers and wives.

FINALE

◊

*La poésie droit avoir pour but
la vérité pratique*
Paul Éluard

Manifesto on Ars Poetica

My poetry is exacting a confession
from me: I will not keep the truth from my song.
The voice undressed by the bees;
I will not bar the voice undressed by the bees
from entering the gourd of my bow-harp.
I will not wash the blood off the image;
I will let it flow from the gullet
Slit by the assassin's dagger through
The run-on line until it rages in the verbs of terror;
And I will distil life into the horrible adjectives.
I will not clean the poem to impress the tyrant;
I will not bend my verses into the bow of a praise song.
I will put the symbols of murder hidden in high offices
In the centre of my crude lines of accusations.
I will undress our land and expose her wounds.
I will pierce the silence around our land with sharp metaphors,
And I will point the light of my poems into the dark
Nooks where our people are pounded to pulp.
I will not coat my words in lumps of sugar
But serve them to our people with the bitter quinine.
I will not keep the truth from my heartstringed guitar;
I will thread the voice from the broken lips
Through my volatile verbs that burn the lies.
I will ask only that the poem watch the world closely;
I will ask only that the image put a lamp on the dark
Ceiling in the dark sky of my land and light the dirt.
Today, my poetry has exacted a confession from me.

We Must Crush the Parasite

after Pablo Neruda

We must hunt that parasite, the pest,
until we crush him under our boots;
smoke him out of his hill-hewn palace
into which his desire for death has driven him.
Either stone him down his self-made prison
Down the luminous dungeon or snuff him out,
And let him writhe in the scorching sun.
We must spray him with terrible bullets of verse,
This skunk who has made dark and shady
Transactions with the enemy and sold our land;
Bombard this thing till it is tattered like a rag:
This flea, this swollen jigger, this parasite
lodged between the immense toes of our land,
filled to the neck with our pilfered blood.
We must fearlessly dig our own flesh
and root him out of his secret hide-out;
Hook him out by his shrivelled wasp legs
Swaddled in the London worsted;
Flush out this parasite that wears the image
of a benevolent lion stained with our blood:
Grab his false tail and chop off
his long claws that have strangled our land,
that have reached every hut and snuffed out the fire.
We must grab him by his false tail
and brain him against Mulanje mountain.
We must be ready with our sharpened pens and inkwells
filled with the blood he has siphoned from our veins
and splash his huge sin all over his overcoat.
We must be ready with hard-hitting couplets
angry with double hatred, furious with love,
tercets exploding with thrice the violence
of this terrible lion.
We must load them with monstrous images

of fierce grotesque lizards always ready to strike.
We shall train our polished steel muzzles on him,
let the hand grenades of flaming metaphors
get him right in the gut, and ravage this handful of dust.
We must rout this terrible *Chitute*[1] today;
We must crush this parasite today.

Providence, RI: 16 November 1982 and 8 April 1983

---

[1] *Chitute* the ugly mouse that amasses food

Acknowledgements

The author and publishers would like to thank the following for their permission to use copyright material.

Paul Green Publishers, Peterborough, for the 'Dusk' and 'Dawn' sections from *Nightwatcher, Nightsong* which was published as the first booklet in the *Dangerous Writers Series* (1986); Ravan Press, Johannesburg for the poems: 'Going Back Patiently,' 'A Love Poem for My Country,' 'A Hanging,' 'Walking Under a Tall Building,' and 'A Grain of Salt' from O *Earth, Wait for Me* (1984); Wesleyan University Press, Connecticut, for 'Those Makheta Nights' from *When My Brothers Come Home: Poems from Central and Southern Africa* (1985).

The other poems were originally published in the following journals: 'A Monument to a Tyrant' in *Pig Iron # 15: Third World* (Ohio); 'A Poem for Martyrs' Day' and 'Nightmare' in *Bomb* (New York City); 'Going Back Patiently' in *Odi* (Limbe, Malawi); 'A Love Poem for My Country' in *New Classic* (South Africa) and *Black Scholar* (Los Angeles, California); 'Nightfall' in *Illuminations* (Isle of Wight, UK); 'This Island Now' in *West Africa* (London) and *Pig Iron # 15;* 'Manifesto on Ars Poetica' in *Black Scholar; Paper Air;* 'A Hanging' in *Contact II* (New York City); 'Those Makheta Nights' in *Cencrastus* (Edinburgh, Scotland); 'Wizard' in *West Africa* and *Bomb;* 'Atlantic Crossing' in *Hantu* (New Hampshire, USA); 'Shrapnel' in *Black Scholar;* 'Night Exodus' in *Ariel* (Calgary, Canada); 'Soweto Child' in *Orbit Magazine* (Lusaka, Zambia); and 'We Must Crush the Parasite' (formerly 'We Must Crush the Cockroach') in *Poetry Review*.

www.ingramcontent.com/pod-product-compliance
Lightning Source LLC
Chambersburg PA
CBHW020012050426
42450CB00005B/442